"*A wonderful, moving story. Inspired.*"

Sheikh Mohamadu Saleem
National Council of Imams

"*A lovely sense of humour and a fantastic philosophy of life*".

Sister Giovanni Farquar RSJ
Commission for Ecumenical & Interfaith Relations

"*An inspirational story of courage and hope. As Senator Robert Kennedy once said: 'Each time a man stands up for an ideal, or strikes out against injustice, he sends forth a tiny ripple of hope. And, crossing each other from a million different centers of energy and daring, those ripples build a current which can sweep down the mightiest walls of oppression and resistance.' This was Lolli Fleischmann.*"

Vic Alhadeff
CEO - NSW Jewish Board of Deputies

"*Brilliantly captures those terrible times when the world went mad*".

Andrew Havas AO
Courage to Care

Lolli's Apple

Published by

AK.A. Publishing Pty Limited

303 Edgecliff Road
Woollahra 2025
Sydney, Australia

PO Box 2135
Strawberry Hills
NSW 2012
Australia
Phone: +61 02 9326 1499
Fax: +61 02 9328 2730
Email: admin@akapublishing.com.au
Web: **www.akapublishing.com.au**

ISBN   97809804530-3-4

Editor: Graeme Leslie Brosnan

Cover: Christabella Designs

Printed in Australia by Griffin Digital

Lolli's Apple

by Tomas Fleischmann

In memory of my beloved father and our lost extended family and to honour my wonderfully courageous mother without whose love and devotion my brother Peter and I would never have survived and flourished.

PART ONE

CHAPTER ONE

The Tin Soldier

I was six years old when I was sent to the concentration camp of Terezin in the dying days of World War II. Sixteen thousand children went through Terezin, but only one hundred and twenty-three survived. I am one of those survivors.

My family lived in a castle in a beautiful farming village in the middle of Europe called Mali Bab. Being born into the class of the landed gentry I had a very privileged upbringing. If the cliché is that someone in such circumstances is born with a silver spoon in their mouth, then I was born with the whole canteen of cutlery in mine. When the winters were severe on our estate we moved to the city of Bratislava where we owned a luxurious apartment in a beautiful, three-storey building with nine apartments – one for each of my father's brothers. During the war, all the apartments were requisitioned by the Nazi party and used as their headquarters.

Mali Bab had been part of Hungary, but after the Great War the Austro-Hungarian empire was carved up and our area became what is now part of Slovakia. Unlike a lot of places our lives were essentially unchanged when World War II started and German soldiers occupied the country. However, by August 1944, for reasons I don't entirely understand, the Germans intensified their hunt for Jews. Our family was very prominent in the district and everyone in the village knew we were Jewish.

There were really only two choices: go into hiding somewhere in the local village, or move to a city and hide there. I remember my mother and father asking, "Do you think you could be quiet every day?" My response was, "Of course I could," but they didn't believe a word I said and with good reason. I was a very lively little six year old and ran around like a maniac most of the time. There were also other considerations which I could not have comprehended at the time and only understood many months later. My father thought that we would be less conspicuous in a big city and so the fateful decision was made to move to Bratislava, the capital of Slovakia, which is located on the Danube River. It is only about sixty kilometres from the Austrian capital, Vienna.

Although we owned an apartment in Bratislava, that was obviously out of the question now, and so a little flat was rented in the suburbs of the city. We loaded up one of the cars and the chauffer drove us to the outskirts of Bratislava. From there we transferred to a taxi for the final part of the journey. It soon became apparent that the few possessions we had brought with us were too noticeable in the flat and they were soon dumped and replaced with more ordinary things.

The flat my father rented was in a small block of twelve units. We were located on the second floor. There was an old man living on our floor and one day he asked me if I cleaned my teeth. I thought this was a rather odd question and asked him why he wanted to know. "Well," he replied, "if you don't, this is what will happen to you," and took his false teeth out. I had never seen false teeth in my life and it was such a fright that I have never missed cleaning my teeth since.

My mother and I went down to the local shop to buy some provisions. The shopkeeper asked where we were from and things like that. He could have been just making conversation and being polite, or acting as an informer for the Germans. You just didn't know. My mother's story was we had come to town for a few weeks while our house was being renovated and repainted. This was something I was told to say to people if I was ever asked what we were doing in Bratislava.

I didn't go to school and when the other kids who lived in the apartment block came home I played soccer with them in the local park. They were all nice kids. Within five minutes we were best mates. I remember going to their flats and playing checkers with them, as well as being silly and running up and down the stairs.

Our family had been living in the flat no more than a week or two, when the Germans arrived. Somebody in the flats must have alerted them that we were new to the area. They drove up in a van, raced up the stairs and banged on the door. To hide our Jewish background we had converted to Catholicism in 1942. Mum had dyed her hair from pitch black to red. We gave false names and produced our false papers and baptismal certificates. All this was to no avail. We were bad storytellers and they did not believe a word we said. The Germans took out their pistols and ordered us downstairs and into the waiting van.

There was deathly silence as we drove off. We all huddled together not knowing where we were being taken. Mother and Father spoke very quietly and softly. They obviously knew that the future for us was very grim, and did not want to alarm me. After what seemed a long time, my father turned to me and held me tightly in his arms. He noticed that I had hidden in my hand one of my favourite toys, a little tin soldier. It was about five centimetres high and I remember its gun was slightly bent. At home I had a whole set of these soldiers and my father and I loved playing with them. My father said to me, "That little tin soldier is the bravest and strongest soldier of them all. You must always try to be the same. It is possible that we may become separated for a while. If we do, you must look after Mummy. From now on, you are my brave little tin soldier."

When I think back on those events I now realise that we made several mistakes which probably made our capture inevitable. It was really suspicious that I didn't go to school. Hitler had outlawed the education of Jews and I had never been to a school even though I was six years old. When we arrived in Bratislava I should have gone to the local school. Also, I shouldn't have been allowed to play out in the street every day. Another mistake was that I think my father should have gone to work. He spent most of his time moping around the flat trying to be inconspicuous. Strange as it seems, people notice that sort of thing.

Many years later we learned that my Aunt Ruth Lovi and her father Oskar went to our unit a couple of hours after we had been taken into custody. They knew it was a bad sign that no one was there, but they had to be careful about asking after us, and so there was nothing they could do.

The van came to a halt. The back door was unlocked by the German Gestapo agents and my father was told to get out. He hugged and kissed both of us, but because he lingered a little too long the guard reached into the van and dragged him out, hitting him with a cosh at the same time. This disturbed me greatly. I had never before in my life seen any violence.

I will never forget the look on my father's face as he left us. It was despair, sorrow and longing all in one. We could just see him wave to us as the door slammed shut again.

The van moved on and after travelling only for a few minutes, stopped again. This time my mother and I were told to get out. We were led into a large room where there were many long benches. There were a number of humourless women in uniform who instructed us in German to take our clothes off. We were body searched to see if we were hiding anything and the pockets of our clothes were emptied. I had a little knife and some string which were taken. My most precious cargo, my little tin soldier, I managed to keep hidden in my hand. Our watches and jewellery were confiscated and Mother had to fill out many forms and sign pieces of paper.

After that we were ordered to dress. We were then put into a cell with other women and children and locked up for the night. The cell was very small. It had a double bunk, a toilet, a hand basin and a tiny table with two chairs. There was a small barred window, but the window was so angled and the wall was so thick that you could not see the sky. All you could see was a dim grey light that told you it was day or night. The door was barred and slid along a track. It was bolted and padlocked in two places. A little later we learned that we were in the women's prison. I was allowed to stay with my mother as I was under nine years of age. Otherwise, I would have been sent with my father to the men's section of the prison.

The next morning we were woken up early. One of the guards called to us angrily and told us to come to the opening in the cell door to receive our breakfast. It was horrible food: porridge that was like glue, two slices of old, stale bread, and coffee that was undrinkable. Before long I would think back on this breakfast as being as good as a feast.

The guard returned to our cell door to inform us that in five minutes time we were going to be taken down to the main square of the gaol. He told us that we must take all our belongings with us as we were not coming back. I said to the guard, "How can we take our belongings with us when you took them last night." He immediately raised his hand to hit me, but for some reason changed his mind and screamed at me that I should not be impertinent, otherwise he would beat me within an inch of my life. "A Jewish pig like you should learn to keep his mouth closed when he is a prisoner of the German Reich," he yelled. The door of our cell opened with a loud clunk and we were hurriedly marched away to the main square where we joined some fifty other people who were just standing and shuffling about nervously not knowing what was going to happen. We were ordered not to speak to any other prisoners and to wait for further instructions. It seemed like we stood around waiting forever before a small bus pulled up and we were told to get into it.

This bus was what we would call today a mini-bus and would normally transport about fourteen passengers. It had about six windows down each side although all the windows were blacked out so the prisoners could not see where they were going. Even as a child it was incomprehensible to me how we were all going to be able to fit into this bus. The guards stood around screaming at us and to this day it amazes me that we somehow did fit in. Everyone seated had a person on their lap, there were children jammed next to the driver, people were on top of each other in the aisle, and the remainder lay on top of the second row of people who were on the laps of the seated ones.

The bus was so overcrowded it's a wonder it could move at all, but move it did and about two hours later we arrived at our destination in a very bad state. As you would imagine it was terribly hot and smelly on the bus and people found it difficult to breathe. My mother and I arrived tired and bewildered, but otherwise fine. Several people were so ill they were taken away on stretchers. One of the others told us that we had arrived at Szered.

CHAPTER TWO

A Brick in the Wall

When we climbed out of that horrible bus I saw a set of large double gates with guards either side holding guns at the ready. As we were herded inside I could see open space in the foreground and rows of barracks at the rear. On entering a large auditorium we were searched again. Once more Mum had to fill out some forms and we were given tags which were tied to our right hand. These tags had our name and number on them, and the barracks that we were assigned to.

Szered, which was about fifty-five kilometres east of Bratislava, was known as a transition camp. It was here that our German captors would decide what to do with us and then send us by train to our final destination. This was a much nicer place than the prison that we had been in previously. The food was a little better. We could walk around and talk to the other prisoners. Before long I found some boys to play with and all seemed fine for the moment.

The majority of the inmates were Jews, although one also saw gypsies, political prisoners and cripples. Every day cattle trains arrived. People were put into the wagons and the trains left. No one knew where they were going. Then new people would arrive and take the places of those who had been sent away. When new people arrived we would ask them if they had seen my father, but we heard nothing encouraging. The days drifted by. One day melted into another as we waited for our fate to be decided.

One wet day I and the other children could not go out and play. Instead, we played hide-and-seek inside the barracks. During our game I hid under a bed near my own. I was waiting to be discovered and the longer I remained there undetected, the more bored I became. Just for something to do under the bed I started to pull at the bricks on the wall. To my surprise one of the bricks moved as I touched it. This intrigued me. It was just an ordinary-looking house brick about three rows from the floor. I crawled out from under the bed, found a fork on a table and crawled back under the bed to try and remove the loose brick. The other children had apparently forgotten about me, so I kept on trying to remove the brick.

Why I persisted I have no idea. I scraped and dug and manoeuvred that brick until suddenly, it gave way and it was out. I reached inside the dark opening with some trepidation as I did not know what to expect. There seemed to be nothing there but an empty space between the two brick cavities. I groped around the empty space with great curiosity hoping to find something inside. As I reached down into the cavity I touched something which moved. I moved closer to the hole so that I could reach further down. My hand touched the object again and I wrapped my hand around it and pulled it out. To my surprise and disappointment it was just a tube of toothpaste. I couldn't understand why anybody would go to all this trouble to hide a tube of toothpaste in the wall. Like most kids, I hated cleaning my teeth, but this seemed quite ridiculous.

I took the cap off the toothpaste tube and squeezed it. Nothing came out. I squeezed it harder and still nothing came out. I was tempted to throw it away, but instead used the fork and undid the bottom of the tube. To my surprise the tube was filled with a tight roll of paper. I pulled it out gently and discovered that it was not just paper, but paper money, and a great deal of it. I reached into the hole again to see if I could find anything else and found another tube of toothpaste. This tube also had money in it. I placed the brick gently back where it came from, crawled out from under the bed, and went looking for my mother. With great excitement I told her what had happened and gave her the two tubes of money. What I had found was a great deal of money. My mother immediately went to see a lady she trusted and told her what had happened. They decided that it must have belonged to somebody who had hidden the money when they arrived in Szered, but were obviously transported to another camp before they could return and retrieve it.

After some surreptitious research my mother and her friend found out which of the guards in the camp were corrupt and prepared to purchase things for us, as long as they were handsomely rewarded. My mother was very wise. Although it was still summer, she had a pair of boots and a sheepskin coat made for me, together with a Russian winter cap. For herself she bought a winter coat together with some other things. She gave money to her friend to buy things for herself and her son. With the money she had left over she bought a walking stick for an old lady, who could not walk without one, some clothes for other people, and cigarettes for herself. I remember Mother enjoyed those cigarettes very much.

In relative terms we were quite happy at Szered. The food was reasonable and the quarters adequate. The guards did not bother us very much and could be bribed for extra privileges. This was how Mother purchased a pass to move between barracks to look for my father. We waited for news about him, but heard nothing.

One morning we found our names on the list of those to leave on the next transport. Mother tried to find out where we were going, but without success. Then she tried to have our names removed from the transport list, but was again unsuccessful. Our guards reassured us that we should not worry, that the place we were going to was a great camp, somewhere safe where we could see the war out. After the war was over we would be all be transported back to our homes. I am certain that my mother did not believe a word she was told. However, she told me that she was happy, that everything was fine, and most likely my father would be waiting for us at the new camp.

Mother managed to find some cold cooked potatoes and some bread from somewhere. We bundled up our meagre possessions and waited on the platform for our train. The guards made us line up so that when the train stopped we would be in front of our assigned carriages. It was raining and miserable. People were crying and upset. A few were saying we were being sent somewhere to die. The guards started screaming at people and sometimes hitting them with their rifles. My mother held my hand. We waited on the platform for hours. Then, we heard the train coming. It rumbled into the station blowing soot and smoke everywhere. There was so much smoke we could hardly see each other. I was frightened. I wanted to go home, back to Mali Bab.

CHAPTER THREE

Mali Bab

I was born at the Koch Sanatorium in Bratislava late in the evening on 27 June 1938. Apparently my father, Morrie Fleischmann, was so excited that when he gave details for my birth certificate he was confused as to the date and thought it was 28 June. To this day I also mix up my birth date as sometimes 28 and sometimes 27 June. My mother's name was Yolanda, but everyone knew her as 'Lolli'. At the time of my birth my mother was twenty-four years old and my father thirty-three. My mother's maiden name was Fleischmann, the same as my father's. They were first cousins. My maternal and paternal grandfathers were brothers. Marrying your first cousin wasn't then considered unusual at all.

Mother was the youngest of four sisters, the others being Ilonka, Adel, and Ethel. They were the children of David Fleischmann and Roza Fleischmann (nee Deutelbaum). Mum and her sisters had French governesses. They played tennis, learned to ride horses side-saddle and went rowing on the Danube. When they were old enough the girls were sent to Switzerland where they were taught among other stylish customs the proper etiquette of how to smoke a cigarette in company and especially the use of a cigarette holder. It was all part of an elegant lady's education. There were lots of balls and parties. The coaches, which were pulled by four Lippizaner horses with bells attached to their necks, were converted to sleighs in the winter.

My father was the second oldest of eleven children: eight boys and three girls, two of whom died in infancy. He was the son of Isidor Fleischmann and Sidonia (Sidi) Widden. The family land holdings were extensive and run by the brothers. The properties were called Fako-Puszta, Fekete Nyek, Palma, Mali Bab, Uj Falu, and Kortveles. Some of them were so large that a railway line came onto the property to take the produce away.

It was my good fortune to be born into a life of wealth and privilege. My mother and father and I lived on a property known as Mali Bab, 'Little Bab'. Our home was a fifty-room castle which was monstrous in size. There were two massive stone lions at its porticos and the castle comprised several wings and numerous empty rooms where as a child I could play hide-and-seek. A short distance away there was a guest house for when we had visitors. This was a relatively large house with its own staff.

The main products grown on our property were sugar beet and tobacco. The sugar beet was grown in rows and between every fourth row a trench was dug. The beetles that attempted to eat the crops would fall into these trenches and were unable to climb out. A tractor was fitted with burners and it would drive up and down the rows burning the beetles, thus saving the crops. I used to love going on that tractor when this operation was being carried out, but the smell of these burning beetles was horrendous.

Also, I was fascinated how the fields were ploughed. There were two steam engines, one either side of the field connected by massive cables. The plough was attached to the cables.

One steam engine pulled the cable to it and the row was ploughed. Then the steam engines were moved the width of the plough and the next row was ploughed. At times these steam engines were so far apart the drivers had special tooting signals to let each other know what they were doing.

The sugar beet was carted off to our own processing factory on the property where sugar and power alcohol for fuel were produced. The alcohol was used to power the farm tractors. What was left over was sold. The head and skin of the beet were cut off and kept in silos and used for fattening cattle. Tobacco was planted in the fields in great rows. When the tobacco was ready for harvesting the village peasants picked the leaves by hand. It was gathered in bunches and then transported to the drying sheds where it was hung out to dry. Watchmen guarded the sheds day and night. When the tobacco was dry it was taken to the cigarette factories which processed our tobacco and turned it into cigars and cigarettes. Other crops such as wheat and barley were grown and we also had cattle, pigs and cows. Milk was produced in commercial quantities. There was also a small winery and my grandfather would take me by the hand and walk with me to the cellars so that he could test the wine. This was just a ploy to trick Grandmother that he was taking me for a walk, but all he was doing was going to the cellar for a little snort.

There were also a carpenter's workshop and a blacksmith's shop on the property. I loved to watch these tradesmen at work, but they obviously thought I was a nuisance, or someone sent to spy on them. Once, they thought of an ingenious way to get rid of me. I was put on the back of a draughthorse which was going around in circles pulling the grinding stone that ground the grain for the peasants' bread. They left me there and promptly forgot about me. I was too small to climb down from this horse and it wasn't long before my governess noticed I was missing and had everyone out looking for me.

I do remember that the carpenters were always fighting with the blacksmiths. They had to work together when making things like a wheel for a sulky, but this often degenerated into an argument with one group of tradesmen accusing the other of incompetence. On one occasion the carpenters made me a little cart which was to be pulled by a goat. They did a very nice job, but I was too young to know anything about goats. They are the most stubborn, the most arrogant creatures you will ever come across. Once the goat was hitched up to my cart, it would take no notice of what I wanted it to do and it would make for the hills. Goats like to climb and as we headed up a steep hill I fell out the back of the cart. The goat returned home without me which created a bit of a panic, but I thought it was all good fun.

It seems that my life revolved around creating as much mischief as I could possibly get away with in order to get rid of my boredom. Although our farm had everything you would ever want, I was the only child in the family. We had coaches and horses. I used to pester my father, grandfather and uncle to take the horse out myself. One time my grandfather and I were in a two-wheel sulky with the coachman behind and the two of us in the front. I kept demanding to take the reins and wore my grandfather down until finally he gave me the reins. He said, "Always keep the reins tight, because if you put the reins under the horse's tail, he will go mad." Well, of course I slackened off and slacked off and did everything I could to get the reins under the horse's tail. Sure enough, all of a sudden the horse reared up and we all fell off the back of the sulky. My grandfather nearly died from fright. That was the only time he gave me a smack.

Our refrigerator was actually an ice chamber at the back of the castle. This chamber was about the size of a room and had been cut into the rock below ground level. It was insulated on the bottom and sides with straw. In the winter ice was cut from the river and put in this pit. The ice lasted all through summer and this ice chamber held the most wonderful delicacies.

The kitchen was in the castle basement and food was brought up to the dining room in a dumb waiter and served by a butler wearing a formal black suit, tie and white gloves. Often, important people, friends and neighbours would come to dinner and occasionally there were parties. There was no electricity, the crystal chandeliers were lit by candles. At times a gypsy orchestra dressed in local costume was called in to provide music.

For fun there were tennis, billiards, table tennis and bowling. A bowling alley which ran along the side of the castle had been constructed by the village carpenters. When we played a peasant boy stood at the end of the bowling alley to return the balls.

The main house had a set of secret passages. If you needed to escape you could follow these underground passages which led into the nearby forest. Sadly, these secret passages were no use to us when the Germans came. Our estate also had its own forest where wild deer used to roam. The family employed a gamekeeper to look after game in the forest.

My father managed the property and his brother, my Uncle Alex, was the salesman. He used to go to Vienna regularly to negotiate the sale of our tobacco and sugar beet. When he returned he often brought me back toys, and one day he came back with a set of tin soldiers. Uncle Alex and his wife Eti had no children, so in a sense I was also their child. After that every time he went to Vienna he would bring me back more toy soldiers and my father and I would set them up and fight these make-believe battles. A table was set up with miniature hills and roads and my father and I spent many enjoyable hours playing with those little soldiers.

My father was even more gentle than my mother. He was the sort of person who would walk around an ant rather than step on it. Dad had a small Zetka 250 motorbike. He used to sit me on the tank and we'd ride out to the fields to see what the workers were doing. 'Morrie', as he was known, was respected and loved by those who lived on the property. Although there was a manager in charge of horticulture my father took a lot of interest in this. He would tear a newspaper into strips on to a plate, wet it, and then put seeds on this and put it in the kitchen where there was light. As the seeds germinated he would label them and discard the ones he didn't want.

Dad was always a well-dressed gentleman, and his favourite sports were fencing and horseriding. I can still picture him wearing a face mask and brandishing a foil while fencing with his friend, Yorsie Prosnitz, down the corridors of the castle. One of my aunts described my father as the kindest person she had ever known.

Once, there was a rat plague in the fields and my father offered the peasants of the village ten cigarettes for every rat tail they brought in. Before long there were so many rat tails presented that Dad had to send to the supplier for more cigarettes.

The family had a beautiful bottle-green Buick motor car with black mudguards and running boards and leather-covered spare wheels on both sides. It was driven by our chauffer, who was separated from the passengers by a sliding glass partition. There was a folding seat behind the partition for me to sit on so I faced backwards as we drove along. Sometimes, when Uncle Alex went to see clients he would take me and Auntie Eti along with him. Alex was the oldest son and lived the most extravagant lifestyle. He holidayed in the Greek islands, went on safari to Kenya in Africa, and was often driven by his chauffeur to Paris and Vienna to go to parties or gamble at the casino in Baden bie Wein. When Alex won at the tables he bought back the most beautiful toys.

Quite regularly I visited my grandparents. Grandpa David was a lot of fun. Winters were very cold with snow sometimes up to the level of the window sills and so I was allowed to sleep in Grandpa's and Grandma's bed. We slept with a doona under us and another doona on top of us. In the mornings Grandma Roza would rise first and later return to the bedroom with a small glass of apricot brandy for Grandpa. He never moved out of bed until he was handed his glass of brandy.

I vividly remember one morning after Grandma got up a small feather floated up from the doona. I started jumping up and down on the bed trying to catch this feather. Seeing my enjoyment Grandpa tore the doona a little to let out more feathers. I was having a great time trying to catch these feathers and before long Grandpa had torn the doona wide open and there were feathers all over the bedroom. The room echoed with laughter as I ran around like a wild thing trying to catch them. Grandpa was doubled over with laughter, but not for long.When Grandma opened the door with a tray and a brandy in her hand, we saw the expression on her face and froze. Grandpa was great fun.

Sometimes we travelled to the spa town of Posteny to swim and relax. After dinner one night at our hotel in Posteny the drummer in the band let me beat the drums during the interval. We regularly went to a stunning hotel in the Tatra Mountains where I learned to ski and watched ice hockey and motorbike racing on the ice. The tyres on the bikes had these sharp spikes on them to give them grip.

My life was a dream. This is how the landed gentry lived before the war and our capture by the Germans. To be a member of this privileged class was a life of joy and plenty. Who could have imagined what lay ahead of us.

CHAPTER FOUR

1944

War ravaged Europe from 1939 onwards, but I lived in a cocoon, protected from everything. I was totally oblivious to what was happening all over the world. While my father and I played with our little tin soldiers, real soldiers and real people were fighting and dying across the entire continent. The sheer scale of the slaughter was incredible. Between 1939 and 1945 between fifty and sixty million people died, about six million of whom were Jews who perished in the Holocaust.

My governess was German with a Czech name, Koyetinska. She spoke to me only in German and I always had to address her in German. She slept in the room next to me. In the morning a maid would run my bath, check the water temperature, and then wash, dry and dress me. My governess would then take me to breakfast where the cook would make whatever was ordered for my breakfast. Then, my governess would prepare the toys that I wanted to play with and generally entertain me and do whatever I wanted. At some point in time during the day my governess would present me to my parents. I would stay with them for a while, until I had made a nuisance of myself. Then, my governess would take me by the hand, we'd wave goodbye to my parents and vanish to another part of the estate. At dinner, I sat with my governess next to me. She'd make me sit straight at the table with a book under each arm so that I wouldn't raise my arms when I was using the cutlery.

At times, when I was naughty, my governess would put me into the spare sugar bin in the kitchen and sit on the lid. She wouldn't let me out until I promised to be good. Also, my governess had a boyfriend who lived in the next village, and if I said anything about her trysts with the boyfriend, I was threatened with the punishment of eating raw eggs with lemon. What a brat I would have become if this life had continued.

By contrast the peasants who laboured on our estate lived in mud hovels with earthen floors. In the centre of their hut would be a cauldron hanging over a fire into which they'd chop potatoes and occasionally a little bit of meat. For breakfast, lunch and dinner they'd all come and scoop food out of the cauldron. Instead of glass, hessian bags covered the windows. They washed in the river which meant they only bathed in summer. There were no toilets for them – they went behind the cowshed and used dry corncob husks to wipe themselves. They froze in winter, boiled in summer and ate little more than potato and corn soup. There were no doctors for them and no medical care. Naturally, there was no union for agricultural workers. They worked from sun up to sun down, six days a week. Their only holidays, apart from each Sunday, were one day at Christmas and one day at Easter. The life span of the average peasant was about forty years.

Our family was considered to be benevolent employers and was very well liked in the district. Throughout the war the local peasants remained solidly loyal. It is remarkable when I think about it. They all knew we were Jewish, but we were never betrayed by them.

From my perspective as a child, the war never touched us at all. Life went on as it always had. For a long time, we were left alone. Our farm produced valuable commodities for the German Reich, and no doubt our conversion to Catholicism in 1942 bought us time.

A Catholic priest personally delivered our new baptismal certificates. He showed my father and uncle how to age the paper so that the certificate looked suitably old if it was examined by the Germans. A mixture of lemon juice and sugar was sprayed on the certificates and they were then placed on the mantelpiece of the fireplace. They started to scrunch up a little and the light brown stains looked good. The entire family received new certificates from the local Catholic parish. In return generous donations of food and produce were made to the church throughout the war. We also gave food to local government representatives, the police, and other visitors.

However, some time in August 1944 our circumstances changed. I don't know what happened, but our luck had run out and it was time to go into hiding before we were all murdered. Having seen what trouble was coming some of our relatives had migrated to Australia. They tried to talk my father and everyone else into leaving, but I think my parents felt the trouble would blow over. Now, it was too late to escape the country.

Grandfather David, Grandmother Roza, Uncle Alex and Auntie Eti went into hiding in the thatched roof of a peasant's hut in Bab. They would have to remain concealed in that roof day and night for the remainder of the war. It was an incredible risk. If the Germans discovered them, they would not hesitate to shoot both them and the peasants who had provided refuge.

My mother and father and I were to be hidden the same way. Preparations were made for this in one of the huts, but at the last minute there was a change of plans. A decision was made that we would instead move to the city of Bratislava and rent an apartment. The plan was to seek anonymity in the bustle of a big city, but within a week or two we had been betrayed, discovered and captured.

CHAPTER FIVE

The Cattle Train to Auschwitz

A train pulled into Szered station. There were about twenty carriages, a steam engine at the front, and a guard's van at the rear. The carriages were old, wooden wagons normally used for transporting livestock. They were absolutely filthy and in a poor state of repair. My mother, whom I adored, said to me, "Remember what your father said. Do not be afraid of anything that happens."

Guards screamed and shouted to us to get into our assigned carriages. There were no steps to climb up. One had to haul oneself inside. The younger men and women could do this, but the elderly and young children could not. If you hesitated you were beaten by the guards. Some of the younger ones hopped down and helped the others into the carriage. The orders were one hundred per carriage. The wagons smelt of human faeces and were probably harbouring every disease known to man and beast. The Germans liked using these cattle trucks because you could fit in a lot more people than in a normal passenger carriage. Also, there were too many windows and doors in a standard carriage for people to escape from. To them we were nothing more than vermin, so we were herded into cattle trucks.

The doors were slammed shut when the guard counted the one hundred allocated to our carriage. We were packed in like sardines. You could only stand. No one could move. It was hard to breathe and terribly hot. People started to cry. Some became agitated and started banging on the sides of the carriage, demanding to be let out. There was absolutely nothing inside the carriage apart from one hundred human beings and one bucket which was to serve as a toilet for all of us. There was no water and no food. Some of the older people passed out, but there really wasn't anywhere for them to lie down.

The train seemed to stand at the station forever. Then, all at once, it started to move very slowly, gradually picked up speed and rattled along. As we passed a point water was sprayed into the carriages. Everyone tried to get a few drops of water as we were all very thirsty.

An older man in our carriage explained that as we did not know how long we would be on this train he had decided to take charge. He said that just because we were treated like animals we did not have to act like animals. This man organised some of the old people to sit down, and children were encouraged to sing songs. This lasted for a little while until fights and arguments started breaking out. To use the toilet bucket you had to go in full view of everyone. The bucket was overflowing, but because the carriage was locked there was no way of emptying it. Night fell and things went from bad to worse. One of the old people died and a man who said he was a Jewish doctor said that it was probably a heart attack. His body was placed in a corner, and it was soon followed by other deaths. The smell was unbelievable. A combination of faeces, vomit, perspiration and death. I quickly learned to recognise the smell of decomposing bodies.

Luckily for me, Mum had brought some food and in the darkness we ate a little saving some for later. We felt bad about not sharing our food, but this was a life-and-death situation. Our journey continued for another day in these appalling conditions. We stopped at a station and through the cracks in the sides of the carriage we saw the station name of Auschwitz.

By 1944 Auschwitz was notorious among Jewish people as being a death camp. In the West, there was very little known about such places, but many of the adults in our carriage knew exactly what sort of place it was. The realisation that we had arrived at Auschwitz struck fear into our hearts. Some began to moan and cry, others were desperate to escape and started to become uncontrollable. So much for the promises of the guards at Szered that we would enjoy our final destination and see out the rest of the war there.

Powerful hoses were aimed through the openings in the top of the wagon. This washed some of the filth out and enabled us to get a little water to drink. Then, a while later, some loaves of mouldy bread were thrown in. Scuffles broke out, but we somehow managed to obtain a small piece of bread. The stench in the wagon was unbelievable. We now had five dead in our carriage. Through the cracks people begged the guards to remove the dead, but they refused. Some questioned the guards what was to become of us, but they said nothing. We waited and waited. Nothing happened. Night fell.

The next morning, the carriages were opened. With guns trained on us we were ordered to stay where we were while they removed the dead. We stood and waited. Then, the strangest thing happened. The carriage doors were closed and the train began to move away from Auschwitz. As the train picked up speed we realised we were going somewhere else. At first we thought we had cheated death if only for a few days. Later, we found out that our lives had been saved because the ovens at Auschwitz had broken down creating the most appalling backlog. There were dead bodies stacked up everywhere and apparently, there were some six thousand prisoners waiting to be processed. When our train arrived with another two thousand the camp leader lost his temper and refused to accept us.

As the train travelled through the countryside my mother suggested to the man in charge that her son, Tommi, who was very mechanically minded, be put to the task of picking the padlock on the carriage. "Our fate is sealed," she told him. "Unless a miracle happens we are all going to die." With that Mother and I were allowed to go to the front of the wagon where the padlocked trapdoor was. Hairpin in hand, I enthusiastically attacked the padlock. All eyes were upon me hoping I would open the trapdoor so that we could all escape. For a whole day I tried and tried, but to no avail. The lock remained as I had found it. However, the move to this part of the wagon was good for my Mother and me. The air was a great deal better and working on the lock kept me occupied. That night Mother and I ate the last of our food. Then we somehow fell asleep on the filthy floor of that wagon, with me holding my little tin soldier in my hand. I dreamed that I was playing with my father on the beautiful fields of Mali Bab. Dreams certainly are suppressed desires, because unfortunately that would never happen again.

When I awoke we were at another station, but I could not see the name. We were hosed again and some mouldy, raw vegetables were thrown in. How beautiful they tasted. How life changes in the blink of an eye. Grandfather David used to tell a story of my eating habits when I was little. Apparently, I was a very fussy eater. One trick Grandfather employed was to beat a drum to make my governess dance. When she started dancing my mouth would open and Grandmother would quickly use the opportunity to pop a spoonful of food in. What I would have done to have some of that food now. The dead were removed again. It's strange how you can become used to such horrible occurrences very quickly. Every day you become harder and your childhood just disappears before your eyes. There was more hosing down, as if we were nothing more than livestock, and the train moved on again.

After six days on this train we arrived at our final destination, Terezin. About two hundred, mostly elderly people, had died enroute. At least their suffering had ended and they had to endure no more. While still in our wagons at the station we were again hosed down. Then, the doors were opened. We picked up our meagre belongings and stumbled into the darkness not knowing what was in store for us.

CHAPTER SIX

Terezin

The town of Terezin lies at the junction of the Eger and Elbe rivers about sixty kilometres north of Prague. In the late eighteenth century a huge fortress, which was named after the emperor's mother, Maria Theresia, had been built and the town grew up around it. When the Nazis invaded Czechoslovakia they converted the fortress of Terezin into a Gestapo prison and concentration camp. Rather than using the term 'concentration camp', the Germans preferred the term 'ghetto', and so it was officially known as 'Ghetto Theresienstadt'.

Initially, Terezin was to be a model camp where foreigners could be taken and shown its humane living standards. Some of the first inmates were elderly Jews who believed they were coming to a spa town given to them by Hitler. They had signed contracts to the effect that they had paid for a place in a 'Home for Aged People' which provided accommodation, board, medical services and recreational facilities.

This was a lie of course. Everything about Terezin was a lie. Those who were brought here in crowded rail wagons after days of cruelty and humiliation were condemned to die. All that had to be determined was when this happened. Jews were brought here from all over Europe. After processing at Terezin they were either shipped to the gas chambers and ovens in the East, or put to work in the camp. Before the war the town's population was seven thousand. When my mother and I arrived the number of prisoners was estimated at forty thousand.

I remember arriving at Terezinstadt as if it happened yesterday. After each transport arrived the prisoners were brought to the administration courtyard and a reception procedure followed. We had to form one long line and a German at the front, who looked like an officer, directed people left or right. Some of the older people were sent to one side and the younger ones to the other. Lolli and I joined the other young people. After being registered in the reception office, everybody had to hand over all their documents and valuables. When they searched us, I kept hidden my little toy soldier in my hand. We were then marched until we came to a large building which said in German 'Shower Block'. Here, we were told to take all our clothes off. The clothes were to be fumigated and then returned to us. Each wagon load of people put their belongings on a cart. The cart was taken away by Jewish prisoners for 'delousing' and we were told they would be returned in twenty-four hours. Then we were herded into the shower block a couple of hundred at a time. We all stood there naked. The doors slammed shut and we waited for the water to start running. Someone screamed out, "We are going to be gassed." Hysteria broke out. People cried and hugged each other. Parents held onto their children. Some women started tearing their hair out, some fainted, some prayed, others beat the walls with their fists. Some lost control of their bowels.

All of a sudden the water started to come out of the shower roses. We could not believe our good fortune. Some of the women started singing with joy. Our lives hung by such a fine thread. There was nothing to dry ourselves with. After our shower we were marched off naked.

We had to form another line and then stood around waiting for several hours. Guards walked up and down the lines humiliating and maltreating the newcomers. The men were issued their prison garb, and everybody received a mess tin, a spoon, and a blanket. There were no uniforms for women and children. Our fumigated clothes were returned and we wore what we had arrived in. Then we were consigned to our cells.

My mother and I ended up in a massive dormitory room with bunks three high all around the walls and a large empty area in the middle. There were more people than bunks and so some doubled up on the bunk and the remainder slept on the concrete floor. This was the first bed we had seen in days. Soup with some bread was served. We were clean. We were alive and felt pretty good. Everyone was in some form of undress, but after swapping and scrounging clothes from each other, a degree of decency was established.

Our hearts sank when we realised there was just one toilet and handbasin for six hundred people. You had to line up for hours to use the toilet. The guards could see that this was never going to work and brought in some buckets for us to use instead. The smell became unbearable. Then I noticed drops of water dripping down on me. As this water continued to fall I said to my mother, "Look, Mama, it's raining inside." We looked up to the ceiling where there were these huge pools of condensation forming. With precious little ventilation and extreme overcrowding it was 'raining' human sweat.

There were quite a few older boys inside our prison. They took younger boys like me under their wing and played with us, teaching us new games. We found boxes and boxes of German forms in our barracks. The older boys taught us how to make paper planes and boats. I took to making these paper toys very quickly. During my time in the camp whenever I was bored I occupied myself by making paper toys for the smaller children. The other children I met spoke matter-of-factly of the humiliation they had received before coming to Terezin. They were forced to wear the yellow Star of David sewn on their sleeves, then expelled from their schools. Jewish children were forbidden from going to school or using a public park. They were only allowed to play in cemeteries.

There was a chronic shortage of food in the camp. What food we had was monotonous and un-nutritious. It consisted of a small bowl of vegetable soup once a day, and a slice of bread. There were few vegetables in the vegetable soup, so it was little better than hot water and tasted like dishwater. Lunch was two cups of coffee and it was the worst coffee I have ever drunk in my life. Without the necessary calories and vitamins we all lost a lot of weight. If you dared to complain you got nothing.

Some of the men were given work in the kitchen and store area, and their tasks included taking the food scraps out in a cart. Being quite enterprising, the next day they stole a heap of food, stashed it under the garbage on the cart, and smuggled it into our barracks. Some old, empty suitcases were found and the food was put inside the cases. The men told the guards that they had clothes to give to us and wheeled the cart full of food inside. It was hidden until night time and then distributed. We all received some of the food. It wasn't much: we were given a small jar of jam which we had with our bread ration, but we ate it with great joy.

Unfortunately, one of the guards found some of the jars in the garbage from our barracks and the theft was discovered. Everybody and everything was then searched, but luckily there was no food to be found. It had all been eaten. The guards demanded to know who had stolen the food, but no one came forward. The punishment for our barracks was no food for three days. After the three days the guards again asked who had stolen the food, and again no one came forward. We were told that until the thieves who did it owned up, there would be no food for anyone in our barracks. "You can all starve to death," we were told.

This became a desperate situation, especially for the elderly, the women and children. Thinking they would probably get a stretch of solitary confinement or a few days loss of rations as punishment, the culprits decided to own up. The two men were taken away. About an hour later we were told to leave the barracks and follow the guards. We were led to a small area beside what was known as the Small Fortress. Our two 'Good Samaritans' were tied to steel rings on the wall. A squad of German guards lifted their rifles and on the count of three the men who had stolen the food were shot. This was a frightening experience for all of us. My father had given me an air rifle for my sixth birthday. The gamekeeper who looked after the deer on our estate had taught me the first lesson of handling firearms – never ever point a gun at anybody. What a terrible thing it was to shoot those men. I realised that living in Terezin was going to be an ordeal. After the execution we were addressed by our Commandant who told those assembled that this is what happens if you do something wrong. As time went by we found out that this sort of punishment happened quite regularly. There was a purpose-built area for hangings, and executions by firing squad.

One day melted into another. Life was hard. The food and accommodation were horrible, but the worst part for me was the boredom. There was so little to do. They don't build playgrounds in concentration camps. Then came news that my mother and I were to be relocated. Announcements like this were always a cause of great concern.

The Germans were not to be trusted and a promise of a move to somewhere more comfortable where we could sit out the war in safety usually meant a train ride to the ovens of Auschwitz.

CHAPTER SEVEN

The City Ghetto

The people who had been on our train with us were assembled and then split up. We were put in a group which comprised women and children. The rest were then loaded onto a cattle train and sent East, where they all perished. Under the watchful eyes of the guards we were marched to a building on Bahnhofstrasse (Railway Station Street).

We were split up and our group of nine women and seven children were shown into a small room on the third floor a few doors away from the communal bathroom. There were ten double bunk beds in the room. The mothers occupied the bottom bunks and their children the top bunks. In the middle of the room was an old pot-bellied stove which didn't work. Our room was on the corner of the building overlooking the end of the railway line. Several times German officers and guards made the comment that we were living in a 'model camp'. Later, we learned that mothers with children were given a temporary stay of execution and allowed to stay in Terezin because the German propaganda people wanted to show the Red Cross how humane they were. This meant, for the time being at least, that we would not be sent East to be exterminated.

Apparently, we had been grouped in order of our social standing at the time of our capture. People like us, who were landed gentry, were allocated better accommodation than others. This was one of those inexplicably bizarre German classification practices. Compared to what I was used to, our room looked very shabby. It was filthy, the paint on the walls was peeling, the electric light did not work, and the smell was putrid. The mattresses were riddled with bedbugs which bit you constantly. Without a working stove the cold was unbearable. Compared to any other concentration camp, this accommodation was sheer luxury. However, it was not good enough for my mother. After a few weeks she and some of the women in our room became good friends. My mother told the other women that we deserved better than this and that if we had to stay in this horrible place we may as well be more comfortable.

God forbid that I would describe my mother as pushy, but when she got an idea in her head about something, she could move mountains. With me in tow we went to see the adjutant of our barracks. She knocked on the door, and we were asked in. Speaking German in her most charming, but determined way, she demanded that the adjutant make improvements to our accommodation.

Even now, over sixty years later, my memories of this encounter are so vivid. My governess had been German, so I could speak the language and knew what was being said. It was the most astonishing thing to witness. The German adjutant at first listened in disbelief. Then, he went red in the face and I thought he was going to explode, and explode he did. He screamed at my mother. I was terrified we were going to be taken out and put in front of the firing squad. However, this officer had met his match when it came to my mother. At the time she was thirty years old, very pretty, and the way she spoke exuded class and a cultured upbringing.

When the adjutant stopped to take a breath she calmly explained to him that if he really wanted to impress the Red Cross, with his 'model camp', then he should make our accommodation a 'model room'. "When the Red Cross inspectors come, they'll want to see an example of the living quarters," she explained. "What will you show them? Our filthy room?" Mother suggested that the room should be fumigated to kill all the bugs, that we be given new mattresses and beds, that the lights be fixed, and a new stove be installed to provide adequate heating. Then, the room could be painted. Perhaps a pale yellow would be suitable. None of this was really any trouble and the adjutant's superiors would be impressed when the Red Cross spoke very favourably about what they saw. What a moment it was. Here was my mother, the 'vermin' of the Reich, with brat in tow, charming this irate, but bewildered officer into submission.

The following week we were moved out of our room to temporary premises while the work was carried out. My mother became a hero that day. For the sake of deceiving the Red Cross some other rooms were also remodelled. Everybody was envious of our room. With death and depravation, sickness and suffering all around us, we lived in an oasis. How lucky we were. I think what my mother did was an incredible act of courage. We knew what those Germans thought of us, but her actions were instrumental in our survival.

I have forgotten most of the names of the others in our room, but I will forever remember their faces. Mary Fiala and her mother Gizzela became life-long friends. Also, Vera and her mother were great companions at this time. I was very disappointed to learn that in our rooms there were only two boys: myself and a boy a little younger than me called Egon. The rest were girls. Who needs girls? They are nothing but pests.

Although we had been baptised as Catholics, once we had been arrested that pretence was not continued. We were put with Jews and thought of as Jews. The majority of the prisoners were Jewish, but there were also gypsies, homosexuals, and political prisoners at Terezin, each required to wear a special armband. They were separated from us and put in a different area altogether.

Most prisoners lived in the big barracks or in town houses including attics, cellars and open yards. Men lived separately from the women and children. They had the worst of it. Their common rooms were immensely overcrowded. In the barracks where the majority of the prisoners were housed there were several hundred people in one room. These rooms were unheated and there was no running water or sanitary facilities.

The camp was run by the SS. A Council of Elders represented the prisoners and was responsible for administration. However, they were obliged to follow all orders given by the SS command. The SS enforced order through terror and were backed up by guards known as Protectorate policemen. Unlike the SS, some of these guards treated the prisoners with respect and helped them when they could. Also, unarmed ghetto guards, organised by the prisoners, helped to keep discipline and order in the overcrowded camp. Some of the inmates were more dangerous than the Germans. To survive some inmates ingratiated themselves with the Germans by informing on people. You had to be very careful about what you said to anybody. I could speak a reasonable amount of German, but my mother cautioned me,

"Don't let them know you understand German. You say nothing."

People with official positions in Terezin wore caps which distinguished them from each other. To pass the time I would watch the daily parade of officials as they walked by. A high cap with a badge and one or two yellow stripes was a ghetto cop. Firemen wore a distinctive forage cap. If you met a man in a white cap you would try to get into his good books, because this man would be a cook. If you made his acquaintance, you were not likely to die of starvation. But you had to be careful not to mistake the corpse bearers for the cooks, for they wore similar caps. If you saw a beret with a little stem on the top, you knew at once that the person was an inhabitant of the barracks where young people were lodged.

To say life in Terezin was strange would be an understatement. Despite the oppressive rules under which we lived, we were permitted to participate in cultural activities. Many outstanding personalities from the spheres of culture, science, and political life were in captivity in Terezin. They arrived from occupied countries from which Jews had been deported. Although our living conditions were atrocious people made the conscious decision to live like human beings rather than yield to the fear of an unknown future. Literary evenings were organised, concerts and theatre performances staged and lectures delivered. There were productions of *The Kiss*, Mozart's *The Marriage of Figaro,* and *The Requiem* by Verdi. My mother took me to a performance of *Brundibar,* an opera for children and performed by children in the camp.

Sometimes these productions were disrupted as performers were sent East to the gas chambers. New prisoners took over the roles and the performances were resumed. Some painters were given work in the cartography department where they were used to make maps. They had access to all the paper and paints they needed and used these materials to draw scenes of what was happening in the ghetto. Their paintings were discovered by the Germans. They were accused on making false propaganda and put on a train to Auschwitz.

Some of the older girls operated a sort of informal kindergarten where we did things like drawing pictures using stolen paper. My mother, Lolli, had been petrified of mice all her life and I remember drawing mice with swastikas on their sides just to tease her. One of the girls made a paper well which we danced around singing, "Ding dong dell, Hitler fell in the well."

Everyone over the age of fourteen had to work. The exceptions were old people, cripples, the sick, and pregnant women. Unfortunately, people who were in this category were usually disposed of quickly. Having a job had certain advantages, such as better food rations, and protection from being transported to the East. Some were employed producing essentials for the war such as ammunition boxes and military uniforms for the army. Prisoners also ran the administration of the ghetto, built basic sanitation, lengthened the water supply pipelines, and built the railway siding from Bohusovice to Terezin. They also built the crematorium in which the bodies of many of their friends were disposed. For obvious reasons, the most sought after work was in those areas where food was prepared – the kitchen and the bakery.

The food situation was very bad simply because there was never enough food. The prisoners who worked for the Germans received a larger food ration, but even that was not enough. The old, unemployed prisoners suffered the greatest hunger because their food rations were the smallest. They usually waited by the servery and kitchens hoping that at least some soup would be left over. Everyone was exhausted and susceptible to disease due to these food shortages.

Two of the ladies from our room worked in our area kitchen. When we lined up for our evening soup, Mrs Fiala would scoop from the bottom of the soup cauldron and give us chunks of potatoes and vegetables lying on the bottom. When others gave you soup they skimmed from the top and gave you little more than water. A scoop from Mrs Fiala was a lifesaver. Occasionally, Mrs Fiala and the other lady, whose name I have forgotten, would steal vegetables, hide them in their clothes and bring them back to our room. Had they been discovered, they would have been shot. We would hold them against our little stove and cook them, or just eat them raw. Little things like this helped to keep us alive.

As the oldest 'man' in our room I was responsible for looking for opportunities to find food or anything that would make our lives better in the camp. With this constantly on my mind I kept my eyes open and noticed a kitchen used by German guards. Outside this kitchen there were bins for scraps and garbage. The vegetable scraps were saved for garden compost, but to me they looked okay to eat. At night I went back with a bag and filled it with all the vegetable bits I could find – the ends of carrots, bits of cabbage leaves, potato peelings and so on. This was great food and I went back every night and took more. I knew the punishment for stealing was usually the firing squad. Sometimes, I would find a whole carrot, or a whole potato in the bin and wondered if the kitchen staff knew what I was doing this and put these vegetables in the bin for me. I would like to believe they did, but I will never know. One night one of the guards fired a shot over my head. I'm sure it was done to frighten me, which it did. But only for a few nights. I went back and kept on stealing vegetable scraps for quite a while. Then, others found out about it, and before long there was nothing left over.

There were random inspections of our rooms. If you had food, money or cigarettes, or a multitude of other forbidden things, you were in big trouble. If the SS were in a bad mood, which was nearly all the time, you would be sent to the firing squad. If they were in a good mood, you might have your food ration withdrawn and be given hard labour.

About once a month we were herded into the delousing station and laundry. Here our clothes were taken from us, and placed into a gas chamber where they were gassed with 'Ventox' which would sterilise the clothes. Mattresses were also treated the same way. While this was being done we just stood there naked. This would go on for several hours. After the clothes were washed and fumigated they were given back to us wet – winter or summer – it made no difference. Think about that – putting on wet clothes in the middle of a Central European winter. People developed chills and pneumonia and died as a result. More often than not we did not get our own clothes back. We knew this was done to break our spirit.

Like most kids I hated anything scratchy and complained to my mother about the horsehair blanket I had which was dirty and prickly and scratchy and riddled with bugs. You would not believe how big these bedbugs were. They were like little beetles and when you squashed them they made this horrible smell, worse than anything.

Sometimes, I used to get them, squash them, and drop them down the backs of the girls' necks. Wonderful stuff. One night, to get rid of the bugs in my blanket my mother went outside, laid it out and covered it with snow. The next morning we recovered the blanket and it was bug free.

Doctors and nurses who had been imprisoned cared for the health of the prisoners as best they could. A hospital was established in the camp, although it had only the most primitive instruments and hardly any medicines. There was a chronic shortage of things like medication, bandages and disinfectants.

I woke up one morning complaining to my mother that my left ear was very sore. We went to see one of the doctors we knew. He thought it was a middle ear infection, but had no medicine to treat the problem. It was extremely painful. My mother put hot packs on my ear, but it didn't seem to make much difference. I endured this constant pain for about a month, and then it got better. However, it left me with a ringing sensation in my left ear, something which cannot be fixed and has stayed with me every day of my life. That ringing noise in my left ear is a constant reminder of my time at Terezin.

One day the whole barracks was assembled. The officer in charge explained that very important visitors would be coming to the camp and that if anyone said anything bad about the camp or their guards, they would face the firing squad the next day. It was reign by terror. A few days later a convoy of vehicles arrived bearing the Red Cross flag. The inspectors toured only our section of the camp and came and looked at our room. The German officer in charge was praised for the standard of care.

Once I was walking in front of one of the residential blocks when something fell with a big 'plop' in front of me. It was a little parcel. I picked it up, opened it, and found inside a watch, jewellery, food and some money. I knew it was dangerous to have these goods found on you, but ran back to our room and gave them to my mother. This was the second time I had found money, and the others called me 'Lucky Tomas'. The blackmarket was rife in Terezin and Mother and the women knew which guards could be bribed. With the money I had found they bought more food, clothes and some cigarettes.

It still amazes me that the mothers took the risk of facing a firing squad for a couple of cigarettes. Old habits die hard.

CHAPTER EIGHT

Peter

The worst moment in my short life happened on 16 February 1945. I woke up early in the morning to discover my mother was not in the bed we shared and not in our room. She was nowhere to be found. I immediately feared that the Gestapo had taken her and I would never see her again. This happened all the time – people just vanished never to be seen again. Normally, I was quite calm, but when this happened I lost it completely. I knew that I could never survive without my mother. The ladies in the room tried to console me. They told me that my mother was fine. She had been taken to the hospital to have a baby.

I had no idea she was pregnant. Actually, I was too young to know what pregnancy was. When the ladies told me this I demanded to see her, but they told me that I was not allowed to see her until she was better. Of course I did not believe a word they were saying. Although my mother had never told me a lie, I was convinced this was a whopper. Why would she tell anyone a lie about having a baby. I was hurt, frightened and worried that I would be left alone in the world. I was distraught and wanted my mother.

This went on for several days until Mrs Fiala told me we would go and see my mother. I could not believe what I was hearing and became very exited at the prospect that she was still alive. We walked over to the makeshift hospital. Most of the staff were Jewish prisoners who had been doctors and nurses before the war. The Gestapo, however, were in charge of the hospital and refused to let us inside. We might have germs and it was safer for the patients if we stayed outside.

Mrs Fiala spoke to the hospital staff and then we went outside and stood in the snow and waited. Then my mother, who was on the third floor, came to the window and waved to me. Oh, what joy it was to know that my wonderful mother was alive. I was so happy I was nearly jumping out of my skin. She leaned out the window and told me she loved me and that I had a little brother named Peter. To me, she looked like an angel whereas the reality was that she was little more than skin and bone. She was at least half her normal body weight and her teeth were all loose from lack of vitamins. Giving birth to a child in a malnourished state in such primitive facilities would have been an incredible ordeal. It wasn't until much later that I learned that my mother was close to death after she gave birth to Peter.

Mother asked me to be patient and to be a good boy. She would be back in a few days. I felt ashamed at all the naughty things I did to worry my mother.

Then she did something I can never forget. Lolli broke an apple in two and threw half down from the hospital window for me to eat. What a wonderful treat. I can still see that piece of apple falling through the air and landing in the snow at my feet. It was the first piece of fruit that I had eaten since leaving home. The doctors had given Mother that solitary piece of fruit for sustenance. It was all there was, and she had given half of it to me. There is no greater love in the world than a mother's love for her children. Of course as a child you cannot fully appreciate this.

Of the three hundred and fifty children born in captivity in Terezin, only twenty-five survived. Some of the children who died were used for medical experiments. Some had their heads smashed against the hospital wall, others died from hunger or disease. My brother Peter was lucky on two counts. He was born towards the end of the war, and also he matched Hitler's criteria for the children of the Aryan master race: he was born with blue eyes and blond hair. Perhaps that made a difference to the Gestapo animals who ruled our lives.

After about a week, Mother brought Peter back to our little room. All the ladies rallied around to help. My mother was still very weak. She had a high temperature and no milk to feed her baby. Another woman from our room had given birth to a baby around the same time. I can't remember her name; just that she was Vera's mother. She breastfed Peter as well as her own baby, and in doing so saved my little brother's life.

From the moment Peter came into our room he screamed nonstop, day and night, driving everyone nuts. I loved him, I was very protective of him, but at times I would have happily thrown him out of the window for a little silence. Poor Peter. He was constantly hungry and not very well. The Germans meticulously documented his birth weight and when you look at those records now you can see that when he was born he weighed 2.65 kilos, but day by day his weight dropped.

Obviously, my mother's pregnancy had been one of the reasons why my parents decided to leave our village and move to Bratislava. As well as needing medical care, it would have been impossible to hide a baby in the roof of a peasant cottage. Now, we were in this hell hole and Father had no idea he had another son. We missed Father and wondered what had become of him. Mother was certain that he would be okay. He was a brave man, and clever. He would survive.

Meanwhile, his older son was rarely brave, and occasionally stupid. I was a child, and every now and then did childish things. Unfortunately, doing something childish in a concentration camp could have the most profound consequences. One day I was out playing with a group of boys when one of the older boys dared me to 'pin a tail' on one of the SS guards. Obviously, this was a terrible thing to dare anyone to do, but I was too young to know this. Not wanting to look like a coward and wanting to impress this bigger boy I immediately decided to do as he had asked. Looking back on it now, I cannot believe that I was so stupid to fall for the dare. The boy handed me a piece of rope combed out at the end. When an SS guard walked past I went up behind him and pinned the tail to the back of his jacket. Then I ran back to the others.

Unfortunately, the tail was fairly long and started to bang on the back of his legs as he walked. After a few steps he realised what was going on and went completely out of his mind. He saw we were laughing and ran towards us screaming in German, "I will teach you little Jewish fuckers to mess with the SS." His face went red with rage. "Who did this?" The older boy who had talked me into doing it pointed at me. The SS guard must have thought I was too young to be the sole culprit. He picked me up by the scruff of the neck and said, "Who told you to do this?" I pointed to the older boy and replied, "He did." With his boot the guard kicked my backside as hard as he could. Then he walked over, grabbed the big boy and dragged him away. We never saw him again.

I tried to be brave, like the little tin soldier in my pocket. However, the toy soldiers I played with and the battles I fought with my father were nothing like the SS. There was no honour and chivalry and glory on the streets of Terezinstadt. I treasured that little tin soldier, but somewhere amid the brutality it was lost.

CHAPTER NINE

Spreading the Lime

As the months of 1945 went by life in the ghetto was marked by new tragedies. As the Russian and American armies advanced thousands of prisoners were evacuated from concentration camps in Germany and Poland and sent to Terezin. Trains came and went right under our window. Mother and I watched the trains arriving hoping to get a glimpse of my father. The wretches who disembarked were starving, sick, miserable and often half-mad.

One transport I vividly remember arrived from Auschwitz. There were over a thousand prisoners and these poor people must have been in Auschwitz for a long time. They arrived in the middle of winter. Everything was covered by deep snow drifts. They were all naked, apart from those few who had managed to find a blanket. They looked sick and starving. These people were just skin and bone. Most were too exhausted to move. They were in a shocking state and were called the living dead. Those who could, wandered aimlessly about the station platform. The ladies in our room had some old stale bread that they threw out of the window to these poor starving wretches and all hell broke loose. They all scrambled for the bread fighting with each other to get to the food. It was a horrible sight. The guards below raised their weapons and forbade anyone from giving them food as they were killing each other for it.

Over the next few days these prisoners remained where they were at the railway siding. They were never fed and either froze or starved to death in front of our eyes. As they died they were taken in carts to the Terezin crematorium. Almost all the Jews from this train died and we could do nothing for them. Towards the end of the war about thirteen thousand prisoners arrived in an already overcrowded Terezin having been evacuated from concentration camps in the East before these were liberated by the Russians.

According to the German authorities there were no crematoriums at Terezin, but this was a lie. The tremendous concentration of prisoners and the lack of proper medical care caused frequent outbreaks of infectious diseases such as spotted fever, diarrhoea, tuberculosis and typhoid fever. Often these outbreaks assumed epidemic proportions. In Terezin alone there were thirty-five thousand deaths.

At first, the dead were buried in a cemetery outside the fortifications in the lowlands of Bohusovice. When they started to run out of room a secret crematorium was built to burn all the dead bodies. We knew this was happening when it started 'snowing' black flakes. Mother said to me, "They're burning the dead people." The ashes of our poor people were belching out of the crematorium chimneys and falling on us like snow.

I recall one man wiping his hands over his face repeatedly as he could not stand the feeling of even a single ash falling on his face. He was obviously going insane, but I was too young to know what madness was. Whenever children saw this man they used to make fun of him, imitating his actions.

When the ovens could no longer cope with the volume of bodies, large pits were bulldozed outside of the prison and the dead were thrown into these craters. Young boys were ordered to go into the pits to spread lime on the bodies. I was one of the boys selected for this task. I used to play football with some of the other boys. For a ball we used rags tightly knotted together. One day we were having a game and as we played a guard became more and more angry with us. He became so infuriated at what we were doing that he couldn't stand it any more. The guard marched over and as punishment for playing football we were sent down to spread the lime.

Other prisoners would stack the bodies into the pits and after a layer of bodies was put down we would then walk on the bodies and sprinkle lime everywhere so that they would decompose more quickly. The reason small boys were chosen was because we were light and would not sink into the partly decomposed bodies as we walked across them. My first job at the age of six. This was frightening stuff for a little boy.

After we had spread the lime they would put down another layer of bodies and out we would go and cover those with lime. Once, I stepped on a dead person's chest causing air to come out of the mouth in a horrible rasping sound. I jumped into the air with fear. I don't think I was ever more frightened than at that moment. This was horrendous work and not without other hazards. Because we were constantly spreading lime, we ended up with lime burns on the exposed parts of our bodies. To this day I still have the burn marks on my legs from that lime.

Thousands of children were sent to Terezin, some with their parents or a parent, and some as orphans. The Youth Care Department, which was run by Jews, did everything possible to make us children feel secure and protect us from the everyday realities of Terezin. Contrary to the Nazi orders, efforts were made to give children a basic education. Older children wrote stories and poems, and made paintings and drawings. Some of these drawings are the only evidence that these children ever existed. A few poems and some drawings are their only legacy. But while I live the memory of those children will never die.

Many years later at a Child Survivor Meeting I met another survivor, Eva Steiner, who was in the same barracks as me. She was only four years old at the time and remembered me as this tough little dark-haired boy who ran around the camp like a maniac. While so many of the kids recoiled in the face of such brutality Eva admired my refusal to cower. It was strange seeing this image of myself as a young child through someone else's eyes.

I was always a very independent and confident child and the human mind is a wonderful piece of natural engineering. Mine has a great in-built defence mechanism. When everything was horrible, my mind went to a different place, to dreamland. Instead of complaining about the freezing cold and there being nothing to eat I used to imagine I was back at our farm on Mali Bab sleeping in a beautiful bed with a doona on top. Clearly I was really lucky to have a brain that worked that way.

We saw things that no one should ever see, much less a child: the savagery of the SS strolling the footpaths bashing people at random, human beings harnessed like horses pulling carts carrying corpses, mass graves, bodies hanging from the gallows until they rotted, the ashes of cremated human beings falling from the sky like snow. And everywhere, the stink of death and decay.

As the months went by we saw more and more aircraft, mainly bombers, flying over the camp very high up. Some of them used to drop pieces of aluminium foil which apparently misdirected the enemy radar. We saw planes from both sides, but it wasn't possible to know who was winning the war. At least with the coming of spring, our living conditions became more tolerable, but food was even more scarce than ever.

CHAPTER TEN

Liberation

We woke up on the morning of 7 May 1945 to discover there were no guards. The last of the Germans had vanished. Everyone thought that was strange, but there was always the worry they would come back. In our situation we knew nothing of the war – who was winning – who was losing – and whether it would soon be over.

Then, a couple of days later, on 9 May, my mother's birthday, into our camp walked these American soldiers. Like the Germans they had uniforms, helmets and guns. However, there was one vital difference. These Americans had smiles on their faces. I couldn't speak English, but didn't need to. I knew these men were goodies and the Germans who had fled were baddies. It was as innocent as that for me. The war was over. We could not believe that the day we had hoped and prayed for had at last arrived. We were alive. Soon we would go home to our loved ones.

It was the first time in my life that I had seen a totally pitch-black person. My first contact with an American soldier was a big hug, a kiss on the cheek and a small block of chocolate. I had not seen chocolate for a very long time. Every time I eat chocolate it reminds me of that day in Terezin. I took the chocolate and shared it with my mother. With a cheeky grin I told Mother that for her birthday I had bought chocolate and also arranged for the Americans to liberate us.

Mum and I were so happy. Even though the majority of the inhabitants of Terezin were very sick, everybody seemed to pluck up the strength to smile, and laugh, and enjoy the miracle of what had happened. The Americans brought in rations and medical supplies. Within a few days they were gone and replaced by the Russians who were also very good to us.

It is strange. We had been hungry every day during our imprisonment, and yet when we were liberated and the food started to pour into Terezin, we could not eat.

Apparently, our stomachs had shrunk to the extent that we could not handle food. Some people became very sick from trying to eat. How strange that must sound. At last we had food, but we could not eat it. It was months before we could eat a proper meal.

Prisoners from other camps in the East arrived and brought with them the deadly diseases, typhoid and spotted fever. These quickly spread through Terezin until the Russian army took decisive action to solve this disastrous situation. In the following days the Russians stationed their medical units in the camp. They brought all the necessary equipment, including delousing stations, laboratories and field hospitals.

Quarantine was declared on 14 May and the whole town became one big hospital. Doctors who were former prisoners volunteered to fight the epidemic. During the following weeks hundreds of people died from spotted fever. Even some of the doctors and medical staff were infected and several died. However, thanks to the efforts of these good people, many thousands were saved.

Miraculously, Mother, Peter and I missed out on catching any of these horrible diseases which were raging through the camp. We could do nothing but wait. Through the Red Cross and other agencies Mother tried to locate my father. However, there were millions of missing and displaced people all over Europe and there was no news as yet.

CHAPTER ELEVEN

Home

Towards the end of May the quarantine was lifted and everyone capable of leaving left for home. We found out that there was a train going to Bratislava, and made sure we were on it.

Mother and I prepared for our trip home. There was not much to pack as we had very few material possessions. Basically we owned only what we wore. Most of the other odd bits and pieces we owned were for looking after my little brother Peter. His crib was a drawer from a filing cabinet. His mattress was a pillow case stuffed with rags and for warmth he had a blanket which had been cut down to the size of the drawer. He wore a cut down man's shirt, and on his head a man's woollen sock. Nappies were made of rags pinned together. He had a little square towel that he used to suck the corner of, or just caress himself with it. That was his total world. Peter certainly looked like a child who belonged to the poorest beggar in Slovakia. To Mum and me, he was the greatest miracle and we loved and protected him.

This time we travelled on seats in a proper passenger train. Our journey to Bratislava seemed to take forever. The railway lines had been damaged by either retreating German soldiers or Allied bombers, or both. In a carriage at the front of our train was a gang of men who would stop the train, repair the line, and then we would continue on.

At one point we stopped at a railway interchange. My mother said that I should not move from the seat I was sitting on. Under no circumstance was I to move out of her sight. Poor Mum could hardly cope. She was very weak. Having to look after Peter took all her energy. My adventurous spirit was more than she could cope with. We sat in our carriage waiting at that station for a couple of hours.

Directly opposite us on another railway track was a line of flat-top railway trucks. While I was sitting there I noticed that someone had left behind a pair of field binoculars in one of the trucks. They were just sitting there and didn't seem to belong to anyone. I just had to have those binoculars. When my mother was busy attending to Peter I sneaked away. I opened the carriage door, walked down the steps, and then clambered up on to the wagon opposite our train. If our train started to move I would have time to jump down and get back on board.

I climbed on to the flat-top railway truck and started to walk towards the other end where these binoculars were sitting. Unknown to me there was another boy with the same idea. He was quite a bit older and bigger than me, probably about ten years old. He had climbed onto the train a few carriages behind me and noticed me about the same time that I noticed him. Both of us wanted those binoculars and it became a race. We ran the length of the truck, then jumped on to the next wagon and ran the length of it all the while getting closer to the binoculars. This boy quickly caught up with me and as he reached my side he pushed me off the train. I fell heavily on to the gravel grazing my arms and legs. Just as I was getting to my feet there was a huge explosion. I suddenly realised the binoculars had been a booby trap. The boy who had pushed me off the train had picked up the binoculars which had then exploded killing him instantly. Apparently, the retreating Germans had put devices like this everywhere. I was splattered with the blood of the boy who had been blown to pieces.

When I looked around people had their heads out the carriage windows, wondering what had happened. Not knowing what to do, I ran back to our carriage. I sometimes think of what my mother went through in that moment when she heard that explosion, looked up and saw that I was not in my seat. How my mother would have coped had I blown myself up is beyond my comprehension.

I arrived in tears, covered in cuts and bruises and blood. My mother started to cry. She grabbed me in her arms and held me for a long time. I cannot begin to tell you how badly I felt, causing her all this unnecessary worry. Somehow my dear mother managed to get me through the war relatively unscathed, and now on the way home, when the danger of death was over, I came very close to killing myself through my own stupidity.

We never found out who the boy was who was blown up that day, or if he had any relatives on the train. It was an incredibly sad situation. Even now I marvel at that strange twist of fate. He pushed me off the carriage and in doing so saved my life. After that ordeal no one had to tell me to sit on my seat and behave. I doubt I moved a muscle until we arrived at Bratislava. My mother and I never spoke about what transpired that day.

The next day we arrived in Bratislava. Somehow, Mother had been able to get a message through to the family about our arrival. We left the train and anxiously looked around on the station platform for anyone that we knew. Auntie Eti recognised us standing there and came running over. She was soon followed by her husband, Uncle Alex, as well as Uncle Oscar, Auntie Rosa, Grandfather David and Grandmother Roza, and Ruth who was Edith's sister and my playmate and friend. Everyone was crying with joy that we had come through this murderous ordeal.

I will never forget that day. We were home amongst our loved ones. It was great to be back, but the person we were desperate to see was not there. There was no news of my father. Uncle Oscar gave me a cuddle and asked me if I wanted anything. I thought for a few moments and said, "Could I have some tomato soup, please?" He disappeared for a little while and returned with a bowl of tomato soup. He was an absolute magician. How or where he found that soup I never found out, but I didn't care. Tomato soup was my favourite and this was delicious.

Stories of survival tumbled forth. Grandfather David and Grandmother Roza had spent the last months of the war safe in the roof of one of their peasant huts. Soon, the joy of seeing our relatives was overshadowed by the absence of those who were missing. Ilonka, my mother's older sister, and her husband had been marched out on to the village square and executed on the spot. Of the eleven children in my father's family, all were murdered except three: Uncle Alex and Uncle Emery, and Auntie Chirri out in Australia. One set of grandparents, scores of cousins, and all the husbands were gone. In my family we lost more than seventy-five percent of my relatives, not one of them having taken up arms, or done anything more than being born a Jew.

The return to our property at Mali Bab reminded us that our lives were forever changed. There was to be no triumphant homecoming. The staff had vanished and our beautiful castle was overrun with squatters. Many of our possessions had been stolen. We were not made welcome and went to live with family in the nearby town of Fekete Nyek.

Grandmother Roza's brother was a doctor. He gave up his medical practice for six months to look after us. He came and lived with us and supervised what we ate, prescribed vitamins for us, and gave us exercises to do every day. He also brought a solarium where we had to lie and sunbake for five minutes every day. A special nurse was engaged to look after Peter.

At first there was great expectation that my father would come back. At the end of the war there were millions of refugees crisscrossing Europe. When he didn't return the family engaged lawyers to conduct searches for him. The Red Cross and other agencies were sent photographs and information. We tried not to give up, but days turned into weeks and into months and all hope faded.

Finally, the agencies found somebody who was in Auschwitz with my father, but he did not know what had happened to him. We learned he had been sent direct to Auschwitz after his arrest in Bratislava. The Germans always found a use for prisoners with special skills. However, my father was a graduate of an agricultural college with extensive experience running a large business. What was the use of a skill like that in a death camp. Had he been something more mediocre, such as a cobbler, it may have saved his life. He was thirty-nine years old when he was murdered at Auschwitz.

CHAPTER TWELVE

Flight

We started to get our lives back together when rumours began that the Communist Party would take over Czechoslovakia and practically all the neighbouring countries. This was devastating news for my family because under Communism people with property were considered enemies of the state and had their possessions confiscated. Everything my family had worked hard for over several generations would be lost and we would be evicted from our own home. On top of the recent suffering my family had endured, this would be too much to bear. This time we were not going to make the mistake of waiting until it was too late.

All we wanted now was a little peace and maybe some happiness. As the Carman family were already living in Australia it made sense for the few remaining

Fleischmanns to stay together. Uncle Tibor and Auntie Chirri were happy to sponsor us, and so it was decided that we would move to Australia. All we knew was that it was a vast and peaceful country of seven million people. The fact that it was an island and as far away from Europe and all its problems as it was possible to travel made it a very attractive choice.

As preparations were made for our departure the enormity of what we were about to do started to sink in. We were going to the other end of the world, to a place where they spoke another language, one unknown to me. Even their way of doing maths was different. There was no metric system – it was feet and inches – what on earth was that all about? I had studied like mad to catch up and now it seemed to be a total waste of time and effort as what I had learned would be of no use in Australia. I realised that I would be nearly ten years old and that I would have to learn a language, start school all over again, and find new friends. I imagined that I would be an old man by the time I was finished. I was really mad at the world. Things seemed to be fine in Fekete Nyek. I loved the place. I had made a lot of friends and life was good.

Now, some new disaster was again looming on my horizon. It seemed so unfair.

With the Communists taking power we were forbidden to sell anything. Uncle Alex had to try and sell anything valuable on the black market for a fraction of what it was worth. Another restriction was that money could not be withdrawn from bank accounts. To get around this Uncle Alex was forced to do a deal with the bank manager who wanted half of the family's savings. That way we managed to retrieve half our savings while the thieving bank manager ended up with the other half. Uncle Emery and Auntie Edith caught a ship to Australia six months before us so that when we all arrived we would have somewhere to stay.

The family ordered four large wooden containers to be built. Each container was approximately the size of an average bedroom. Into them went all our remaining possessions: Persian carpets, chandeliers, silver of every description, cutlery, paintings including some of our ancestors, albums of family photographs, kitchenware, bedding, clothing, important papers about the family history, books from our library, lamps, antique vases, electrical goods, some small pieces of furniture, and many other odds and ends. Arrangements were made for these crates to be smuggled to Austria in the wagons that transported tobacco by train from the property. From Austria the crates would be forwarded to Genoa, Italy and from there were to be shipped to Sydney.

I gave a lot of my things to the boys I used to play with. One of the village boys was given my bike, another my Meccano set and steam engine which I cherished. The school was given my beloved projector which had been set up in my bedroom as well as my toboggan, which had its own brakes and steering.

There were some very sad parties, where we said goodbye to friends, and then it was time to leave. The properties, the farm produce and the equipment were all left behind. We travelled to Bratislava, then to Prague and from there to Rome. We lived at the Pensione Italia at No. 18 Via Venecia for nearly four months before boarding a Douglas DC-4 airliner which had been charted by an American Jewish organisation helping Jews who wanted to resettle after the war. There was no such thing as a commercial flight in those days. Many years later I discovered that our five-day flight from Italy to Australia, flying during the day and sleeping in hotels at night, cost per person about the same as the average price of a Sydney house.

We landed in Darwin in the late afternoon. Our papers were checked together with our medical cards. Our flight to Sydney was delayed which meant two days in Darwin. We were allocated an elevated bungalow with no doors or windows, just plastic streamers to keep out the flies. There were gaps at the top and bottom of the walls to allow air to circulate. Of course there was no privacy and everything that was said could be heard in the adjoining rooms. From the verandah all we could see were palm trees and banana trees and some Aborigines wandering about. We were served ginger beer and tea with milk together with Vegemite sandwiches, none of which we had ever had before. It was May and very hot well into the night. My mother said to Auntie Eti, "We have made a huge mistake coming to this country."

The next morning I went downstairs and befriended some of the Aboriginal boys and we started to play a ball game. We didn't need to speak the same language to have a bit of fun with a ball.

The following day our plane arrived. It was an old army DC-3 with aluminium bench seats down each side of the fuselage, and holes cut out of the windows so that machine guns could be fired through them. There was no pressurisation which meant that we flew at a low altitude. Our plane, which by this stage had twenty-four passengers, took two days to reach Sydney and landed four times to refuel. Each time we landed the hostesses put up trestle tables on the tarmac and served us food and cups of tea.

When we arrived in Sydney the Carman family was waiting to greet us: Uncle Tibor (Tom), Auntie Irene (nickname Chirri), Uncle Alex's sister and Mum and Eti's cousin, my cousin Eve, who was twelve years old, and my cousin Peter. It was a wonderful reunion for the family. We had not seen each other since 1939 when the Carmans had emigrated to Australia. I immediately bonded with my cousin Eve, and now nearly sixty years later we are still the greatest of friends. Eve was always like a sister to me.

My family arrived in Australia on 9 May 1948, my mother's thirty-fourth birthday, and coincidentally, the same date we were liberated from Terezin. They took us to Uncle Emery's and Auntie Edith's house where we were going to stay until we found somewhere to live. Uncle Tibor had gone out and purchased seven stretcher beds, bed linen and pillows, and after much talk and celebration we went to bed exhausted.

PART TWO

CHAPTER THIRTEEN

Minegold Farm

A few days later at the age of ten I started at the local school of Bexley Public. The headmaster took one look at me and thought, "What have we here?" I was wearing 'lederhosen', leather shorts complete with long stockings and braces topped off with a beret. To his credit the headmaster said nothing about my clothes. He took out a box of matches from his pocket, spilled them onto his desk and indicated to me that I should count them. I quickly did this and showed him on my hands how many matches there were. "Fourth class," the headmaster instructed and that was it.

I could do all the maths that was set on the blackboard, but for the rest of the school day I just sat there listening. After three months I could speak English reasonably well and began to take part in more of the work.

Uncle Alex decided that we had sufficient money to buy a farm. He met up with a real estate agent by the name of Voss who could speak German and was a farm expert. Voss recommended a poultry farm on the Sydney side of the Blue Mountains. Uncle Alex was very enthusiastic. He took much delight in telling us that chickens were multilingual and understood Czechoslovakian, Hungarian and English.

After looking around he settled on Minegold Farm in Quakers Hill, about forty kilometres west of Sydney. The farm had several thousand laying hens, a hatchery, an incubator house and farm equipment. It was half a mile from the railway station where there was a post office, a butcher shop and a picture theatre. The local school was three miles away. After a look over the farm Uncle Alex and I went to the nearest branch of the Bank of NSW in Blacktown and spoke to the manager. As Uncle Alex only spoke a little English, I did the interpreting for him and the bank manager. Of course if anything went wrong with the sale process it would have been my fault. The bank manager arranged the financing and after seeing a solicitor, the farm was ours.

The day we moved was the middle of summer and it was so hot we couldn't believe it. An even bigger shock was the discovery that our new home on the farm was a tiny, one bedroom house with a small lounge room which included an even smaller kitchen. There was no plumbing or drainage. The toilet was about a hundred metres from the house and consisted of nothing more than a can, which when full had to be emptied and buried. Seven people crammed into two rooms. What a contrast to our lives in Europe, but for the first time in a long time, we were happy.

Devastating news reached us that the crates containing all our precious family possessions had caught fire on the docks in Genoa and had been destroyed. With the loss of those irreplaceable family possessions it seemed as if every link to our past had been erased. All we had now was what we arrived with in our suitcases. A carpenter was employed to convert the garage next to the incubator house into accommodation for Grandfather and Grandmother. This carpenter also built a very large and breezy verandah and installed a toilet and septic tank next to the house. The telephone was connected. Our number was Quakers Hill 2.

Phone calls could only be made from eight until five during the week, and from eight to twelve on the weekend.

For the first few weeks nobody could sleep. Next to sheep, chickens have to be the most stupid creatures in the whole world. If they hear something in the middle of the night they squawk and carry on for ages waking everybody. As everyone knows, at dawn the roosters crow, and thousands of chickens make so much noise that they could wake the dead. Amazingly, after about a month we slept through all the noise as if it wasn't there.

In January I started at Quakers Hill school. Mr Martin was the principal and the only teacher. There were two classrooms: one for kindergarten and first grade, and a second classroom of second, third, fourth, fifth, and sixth grade. Mr Martin would set work on the blackboard for one class, and then go into the other classroom and teach that class. For the first few days I was put into the kindergarten class until he could assess me. After I was assessed, Mr Martin put me into his fourth class. Before the year was out I was moved to fifth class and topped the year in the exams.

I made friends with a few of the boys and we had some incredible adventures together. As we lived quite close to Schofields Air Base my friend Don Pollock and I would often sneak on to the air base even though this was strictly forbidden. The place on the base with the most appeal was the dump where all sorts of treasures could be found. One day Don and I found a pile of small bombs half-buried in a hole. In my wisdom I talked Don into grabbing the bombs and then passing them over to me. As he handed them to me I smashed one against the other. The idea was to break open the bombs, take out the lead, and use it for sinkers for our fishing rods. The second bomb started smoking when I tried to smash it open. I yelled to Don, "Quick come up here – this bomb is smoking. The M.P.s will see the smoke and catch us." After thinking for a moment I then said to Don, "Let's piss on the bomb and put the fire out." The extent of my idiocy had to be seen to be believed.

Piss we did, but of course the smoke only became worse. The military police duly arrived and discovered two boys peeing on a smoking bomb. They could not believe their eyes. Fearing an explosion they quickly grabbed us and dragged us away to headquarters. Our parents were summoned and the seriousness of the situation explained. Of course we learned nothing and within days we were back scouring the dump looking for more trouble.

There was always something happening on the farm. We used to fatten capons, which are de-sexed chickens, for twelve weeks and then sell them to chicken processors such as Steggles and Baiada's. Charlie Baiada was buying from us for a while and consistently we were making a lot less money from him compared to everyone else. His truck was weighed empty, and then weighed when loaded with our chickens yet his load always weighed much less than those of other chicken processors we supplied. Uncle Alex thought something funny was going on and asked me to hang around near Charlie Baiada's house and ask for a lift when Mr Baiada was going to pick up our chickens. I arrived at their place and played for a while and when I saw he was about to leave asked if I could hitch a ride home. I could tell Charlie was not happy, but he couldn't actually refuse to take me.

We arrived at the weighbridge and received a certificate for the weight of the empty truck and the empty cages on it. After that instead of driving to our farm Charlie pulled in at a friend's place. He suggested that I go and play with the children there while he talked to his friend. I did as he asked, but kept an eye on Charlie while I played with these kids. When he thought I wasn't looking he quickly removed from the truck two spare wheels and a massive box, which we later found out had cement bags in it. Then we proceeded to our farm. The cages were stacked with chickens, and from there the truck was driven back to the weighbridge where it was weighed again.

I told Uncle Alex what had happened. The next time Charlie picked up chickens Uncle Alex was waiting for him at the weighbridge. He told the weighbridge attendant what Charlie was doing and they made him go back and get the spare wheels and the box he had taken off. This equalled about the weight of four hundred chickens which is what he was stealing from us each time he came. We never sold to Charlie Baiada again. On this day I was a hero.

I did my share of the work on the farm, but thought up ways to mechanise most of my jobs. We discovered that for the hens to lay more eggs you needed to give them more hours of light. I set about putting lighting into all the sheds. The problem was that someone had to get up at 3am and turn the lights on. I thought about this for a while and decided to cut out the middleman and make an alarm clock switch the lights on. I did this by putting a cotton reel on to the winder of the alarm clock. Then I connected the cotton reel with a piece of string to a mouse trap, which in turn was connected to the light switch. This was all screwed to a board. When the alarm went off the cotton reel started to wind the string on to itself, thus tripping the mouse trap which then flicked the lights on. This system enabled me to sleep in while the chooks starting laying eggs from 3am. It worked for years until an electrician saw what I had done and replaced it all with proper time clocks.

I made many time-saving gadgets on the farm, but the one I was especially proud of was a travelling sprinkler. I made an impeller in a tube that drove a gear box which I had made from meccano parts. That powered a pair of wheels and at the front of the unit there was a cotton reel that would sit on a hose and guide the unit. I could do my homework while the garden was watered.

When my brother Peter and I were given money by relatives I used to swap my pennies for his shillings. I was able to convince Peter that the pennies being larger were more valuable. However, it wasn't long before he understood the value of money and has done very well ever since. Peter was also my tester for the lawn mower. If it wouldn't start I'd ask him to hold on to the spark plug while I pulled the cord. When I did that he jumped in the air from the shock. At least little brothers were useful for something. One day I was reversing the car and asked Peter to help guide me out of the garage. "Peter, tell me if I hit the garage," I said. As I reversed out Peter said nothing and then as I crashed into the side of the garage Peter yelled, "Tom, you hit the garage." Was that dumb or what?

CHAPTER FOURTEEN

Parramatta High School

In my second year at Quakers Hill we were asked what high school we wanted to attend. All the boys were going to Westmead Technical, so I wanted to go there as well. However, Mr Martin had different ideas. He suggested that I should try out for Parramatta High, which was a regional selective school. To get into that school I would have to study hard all year. I remember that when I sat the entrance exam the rest of my class was sent outside. I was left alone in the school room to do the exam. This went on for two days and I managed to qualify for Parramatta High. I was the first 'New Australian' to go to that school.

High school was a bit of a shock to me. There were a lot of rules and regulations. Girls sat on one side of the classroom and boys on the other. There were thirty-five in our class and most of them had been the duxes of their primary schools. To shine here you would have to be pretty good. Every day we had to do the most ridiculous amount of homework. Imagine how pleased I was to find one of the girls from my class on the same train as me every day. She always did her homework and allowed me to copy some of hers. This made my life a lot easier. The Maths and Science subjects I loved, but the other subjects dragged me down. I hated English and History. I had trouble with the teachers as they could not read my writing. It was pretty scrappy. I was ambidextrous and could write with both hands, neither of which was legible. My poor history teacher used to keep me in after school for penmanship lessons.

One day melted into another and probably the most important aspect of school for me was learning how to retain information, to think for myself and developing the general people skills you need for everyday life. I played rugby and water polo. I swam breaststroke for the school. I loved running and the high jump and derived a lot of satisfaction from sport.

At the end of the year there was a dance held at the Parramatta Town Hall. In her wisdom my mother arranged to have me driven to the dance by Uncle Alex, and she tagged along as well. On the way Mum saw a florist and asked Uncle Alex to pull over.

Into the florist she went and asked, "Please, can you give for my Tommy one flower for his bottom hole." Realising she meant buttonhole, the florist nearly choked from laughter and gave us the flower without charge. I arrived at the dance as the only boy with a flower in his buttonhole and was a great hit with the girls. This was even despite the fact that I was a pretty lousy dancer.

To earn some much needed pocket money I offered my services to the projectionist at the Quakers Hill picture theatre. I told Frank Potter that from a very young age I had owned and operated my own projector. He was impressed and so every Saturday matinee I became the assistant projectionist. There was no pay, but the deal was that I could come to the movies with a friend for nothing any time I liked. It was great fun and I loved running those ancient carbon arc projectors. It wasn't long before I was doing all the work while Frank read the paper. He only helped on reel changes which occurred about every twenty minutes. In those days films did not have a sound track on the film itself. Instead, the sound track came on a 78 rpm record. You had to synchronise the record with the film. Many a time what the mouth was doing didn't match the sound coming out and the audience would stamp their feet.

CHAPTER FIFTEEN

A New Life

The two years of study for the Leaving Certificate exam was over very quickly. I thought I had done well in my exams. When the results came out I rode my bike down to the newsagent at 4.30am to look for my name in the lists, but to my horror it was not there. I rang the Education Department and had to go into the city to talk to them. I passed only three subjects: Maths 1 and 2, and Physics. I had been failed on the other three subjects because they could not read my writing. A fee of ten shillings per paper would have to be paid for them to mark my papers again. I was ashamed in front of my family as I had never failed anything before this. After four weeks my results came back. After the re-mark I ended up with four As and two Bs. I had achieved a university entrance pass.

Up until now everyone seemed to be telling me what to do. Now, when I had to make one of the most important decisions of my life, I felt I was being left to my own devices. Like most people, I had no idea what I wanted to do. Some opportunities surfaced, but one evening out of the blue I was told that Uncle Tom Carman may employ me, as his son Peter wanted to leave the business and become a minister of the church.

Uncle's factory, Webbing and Trimming Pty Ltd; operated from premises in Artarmon. It was known in the industry as a narrow fabrics manufacturing plant. The narrow fabrics industry, or small ware, as it is sometimes called, manufactures many of the things we use in our daily lives, but never take any notice of. Things such as shoelaces, belts, hatbands, cords for dressing gowns, labels, garment loops, lingerie straps, zip fastener tape, velcro touch tapes, and all elastic products are narrow fabrics.

When Uncle Tom asked why I wanted to work for Webbing and Trimming I said that I loved mechanical devices and his factory was full of them. I would study the machines and improve them and invent new machines to make the factory the best in Australia. I'm sure Uncle Tom thought I was full of hot air, but he liked my enthusiasm and gave me a start.

That was the beginning of my working life. I don't know what I expected, but I was somewhat deflated when I was asked to operate the little 3F winder that wound the quills for the two curtain tape looms. By morning tea time on my first day I was bored to death with the winder and it was impossible for me to then look into the future and see that I would spent the next forty years of my life in this industry.

I started a course in Textile Technology at the University of NSW. I went out with a lot of girls and holidayed in Surfers Paradise several times with my cousin Eve, Uncle and Auntie. One afternoon a young girl who worked in the office at Webbing and Trimming asked if I would be her partner for a 'Coming of Age Presentation Ball' at the Trocadero. She explained that her boyfriend had broken his leg and would not be able to go with her. It wasn't a great boost for the ego, being brought in as a replacement, but I accepted. We went to dance practice regularly, and started to enjoy each other's company. The presentation ball at the

Trocadero was a great success. We became very fond of each other, fell in love and were married in 1962. In what seemed but the blink of an eye we had four beautiful children and a lovely home.

Whenever I could I played tennis with my friends. One Saturday I was going to Blacktown to play with John Jackson, who picked me up in his very smart MG sports car. While we were driving along some tennis balls rolled from the storage area under the hood to the foot well at my feet. I bent down to pick them up. John must have been distracted and not watching the road. A truck stopped to turn right in front of us and John drove straight under the rear of the truck smashing his head and dying instantly. It was horrendous. I had his blood all over me, but not a scratch otherwise. My life was saved because I was bent over picking up tennis balls at the moment of impact. Again, I had cheated death.

I worked for W&T for twenty-three years, and in 1980 gave notice and started my own company designing and building special purpose machinery. My first project was with Dr Robert Wexler from the Atomic Energy Commission. Using the reverse osmosis process we developed a machine which used specials filters to change brackish water into drinkable water. We entered our device on *The Inventors* program on ABC Television and won on the night and were runners-up for the year.

I worked as a consultant for nearly five hundred companies on various projects such as making theatre screens with special luminosity for wide-screen digital films, medical tapes, artificial veins, tapes for burn victims to make them heal faster, bullet-proof vests, sail lamination techniques, and carbon fibre masts for sailing boats.

I sailed regularly with my mother's nephew, Peter Zalai, but on one particular Saturday it was raining very hard and Peter suggested we should go and look at a motorbike he wanted to buy. I saw a beautiful Honda Racer 250. I fell in love with it and bought it on the spot. I just loved riding my Honda Racer. I loved the freedom. For me the thrill of riding is indescribable.

Many years before this, when I was about eighteen, I had arrived home with a motorbike, but Mum put her foot down and flatly refused to let me have it. "I didn't bring you through the war just to watch you kill yourself now," she complained. Instead, I bought a second-hand Singer 9 which was the cheapest sports car you could buy, and the only one I could afford. The wooden chassis was tired and it creaked and groaned. The doors were secured with timber screws and once one of the doors fell off. The Singer was so unreliable that I had to park it on the hill next to the factory because the only way to start it in the afternoon was to do a roll-and-clutch start. It blew so much smoke that I made a device to redirect the smoke to the front and rear number plates so that the plates could not be seen by the police. Mum later admitted that she often rang the police to ask them to book me for speeding she was so worried I would kill myself.

After I was married every second Friday afternoon I used to visit my mother. One particular Friday I was busy and rang Mum to tell her I wouldn't be able to come and see her. She mentioned that she didn't feel well and that perhaps I should come to see her. Mum quite often said this to make me change my mind. Despite her entreaties I did not go and she died two hours later. It transpired that Mum had this pain in her side. She went to her regular doctor, but he was on holidays.

The locum told her to take two asprin and go to bed. The problem was she had a clot that was travelling slowly to her heart and at sixty-six years of age it killed her. I will never ever forgive myself for this. This wonderful woman who brought me into this world, who saved me from the Germans and looked after me all my life was gone forever. This tragedy was the greatest shock in my life. I felt horrible that I had been so selfish that I could not take the time to visit Lolli when she wanted to see me.

CHAPTER SIXTEEN

Back to the Beginning

A new century ticked over and a new era began. I had started work forty-nine years before and in all honesty I thought that was enough. I had done all that I wished to achieve in textiles so broke the news to my family that I wanted to retire. The annual turnover from when we first started we now generated in three days. At the age of nearly seventy I thought it was time for a change.

As a culmination of my life's work I received a letter from Terry Hennessey, the Director General of The Textile Institute in Manchester, UK, stating that my colleagues worldwide had unanimously granted me the status of Companion of the Textile Institute for substantially advancing the general interests of the industry. Companion membership is limited to fifty living leaders of the world fibre-based community.

A distinguished array of leaders stretching back to 1910 have received such awards. Scrutiny is extremely thorough and the Council acts on the advice of a sub-committee of existing holders of the awards concerned drawn from leaders of the industry from many countries.

In early 2001 my second wife, Caroline, my cousin Eve and her husband, Rex Burchall, and I went to Eastern Europe. In Frankfurt we hired a car and set off through Germany travelling through the beautiful countryside and villages to Prague. On Good Friday we set off for the two hour journey north of Prague to visit Terezinstadt.

It was a bleak day as we approached this desolate town. Freezing rain was falling and for a short time light snow fell. It was with a feeling of apprehension and dread that I walked past endless graves and crosses and monuments to the deceased of World War II as I made my way to the entrance. When the guide learned that I was a former inmate I was given a complimentary pass. We walked over to the old barracks block and prison. The room where my mother and I had been jammed in with six hundred people was as cold and silent as a tomb. Memories came flooding back. I saw the one toilet in the corner of the room. I could hear the screams, the crying, the despair of the sick and elderly. Although the place was scrubbed clean the stench came back to me. I was numb, just taking it all in. I found the small cell about ten foot by ten foot with one tiny high window and a huge steel door where Mother and I stood for several days with dozens of people while waiting to be processed.

Into my mind came the memory of the SS officers and their families who lived nearby, a world away from the degradation and suffering of the prisoners, enjoying such luxuries as a swimming pool. I wondered if any of the former SS guards ever came to relive their past and whether they ever showed remorse for their horrific actions.

We then left the barracks and proceeded to the town. To my amazement I was able to direct our party through the streets and alleys to the block which had been our prison so many years ago. I then located our old room on the corner on the third floor. Directly below was the railway line. Memories just flooded back. It was such a tiny room for sixteen people. Outside, the weather was exactly as I had remembered it: cold, wet and bleak. It was exhausting coming face-to-face with the past like this and I was close to being overwhelmed by it all.

After leaving Prague we travelled south through Brno and deep into the countryside of Slovakia. We travelled along a modern freeway and the village of Bab was not on our map. We saw a service station and pulled in. While we were refuelling I overheard a comment among the men sitting nearby that we must be German. Our rental car had German number plates. When I walked over and addressed them in Hungarian they relaxed and became very friendly. I explained I was looking for the Fleischmann estate and they directed us to the property.

We drove on and suddenly in the middle of thousands of acres of arable turned soil I could see the family castle through the trees. Up the road we went past outbuildings, storage silos, cattle yards, dozens of machinery sheds, dilapidated outhouses, greenhouses and came to a boom gate and guardhouse. Behind the guardhouse was the castle of Mali Bab. A security guard, with a pistol in a holder, came out to see what we wanted. He wore the uniform of the Force Four security firm and spoke a strange Czech dialect I couldn't really understand. He knew some Russian and so I communicated with him in broken Hungarian-Russian-German. I said to the security guard, "This was my home. I lived here when I was a little boy." Even though I was speaking in a mish-mash of languages he was quite overcome and tears welled up in his eyes when I told him my story.

This unfortunate-looking fellow had most of his teeth missing and was wearing a baggy, unironed uniform. He looked as poor as the proverbial church mouse. He told us that he was not supposed to allow anyone on the property, but as he was on duty by himself he would let us have a look around. "I will let you in," he said, "but be quick."

All the doors had electronic locks on them and as we walked from room to room our guard entered his codes. He explained that this was part of his job, to do the rounds every few hours and to press the codes. Never did I expect to be able to enter the estate much less walk around inside the castle. The guard explained that when the Communists had been in power the castle had been used as a laboratory for tobacco-related diseases. Presumably, the authorities thought it was best to bury such a facility deep in the middle of Czechoslovakia. The facility had been moth-balled by the government about ten years before.

It was a truly awesome feeling I experienced as I wandered from room to room with memories of my childhood almost overpowering me. And then I walked up a flight of stairs, down the corridors and into my old bedroom. The tears flowed. It occurred to me that despite the horrors of Terezinstadt, it was the six years of childhood living in Mali Bab which had taught me what a precious gift a family is. My mother, my father and my grandparents were all alive for me at that moment. Grandmother giving my grandfather his apricot brandy first thing in the morning, and my mother relaxing in an armchair, smoking a cigarette. Whenever I remonstrated with her about the dangers of smoking she would say to me sincerely, "Tommi, I promise you. This is the last one." Five minutes later she would light another. I could hear my father fencing in the corridors and see him sitting on his heels playing battles with my little tin soldiers. I could see him together with all my aunties, uncles, cousins and paternal grandparents. Sometimes, when I think of the futile loss of this entire generation the sadness is too much to bear.

For many years, I blamed myself for the death of my father. I felt that they had made the decision to take the apartment in Bratislava because of me, that it would have been impossible to hide a young boy in the roof of a peasant's hut for months on end. Obviously, things became complicated when they learned my mother was pregnant. How could you ever hide a baby in such circumstances.

Soon, our time was up. As we were leaving I turned to the guard and discreetly slipped him one hundred American dollars. "Thank you very much," I said. Again tears welled up in his eyes. "Sir," he said, "there are things in this life that money cannot buy," and he handed my money back. I was amazed that someone as poor as this man would do that. He thought it was immoral to take money for allowing me to explore my childhood home.

We went back to the car and drove off looking for Fekete Nyek. About thirty-five kilometres down the road we saw a driveway and people sitting around a courtyard. One of the old houses had been re-built and was now a pub. I parked our station wagon and as we alighted an elderly gentleman spoke to me in Hungarian and asked who I was. I told him, "I'm Tommi Fleischmann. I used to live here." He then turned to his wife, who was in a wheelchair and said, "It's unbelievable. Tommi has come back from the dead." His name was Stephen Bartalos and when he learned who I was he removed his hat and bowed his head. Stephen had been a farmhand and milked the cows on the property until he was promoted to become an assistant coach-driver for my grandfather. We spent a couple of hours in the courtyard reminiscing and taking photographs.

My journey to Eastern Europe occurred fifty-three years after I left. Another little boy I had known at Terezin took his own life at the age of twenty-five. Quite a few of the other kids seemed to lose the will to go on. Some people allow their thoughts about the past to take over their lives. I never had time for stuff like that. For me, it was different. Although I was devastated that I never had the opportunity to know my father, I also realised that I had been to hell itself and survived. Maybe my mother exerted a critical influence. Maybe I have that inbuilt will to live. I only have two regrets: that there is not enough time in life to do everything I want to do, and that I never had the chance to really know and love my father. My advice to people is to savour every moment. Success isn't measured by just money and assets, it is measured by touching and enriching people's lives.

I have had an incredible life, which I have lived to the fullest. I have tried to do the best I could do in any situation, and hope to have a lot more fun in the future with my wife, Caroline, our children, and our grandchildren. I still ride my faithful Ducati S4 and sail and race on Sydney Harbour with my friends. I have promised Caroline that when I get old I will sell the bike and probably build a car, something along the lines of an A.C. Cobra with a six-litre motor, something to play with in my declining years.

For me, the enduring lesson from the nightmare of Terezin was learned in that unforgettable moment when my mother, Lolli, threw to me from her third floor hospital window, one half of an apple. There is knowledge, and sustenance, and love all around us. All we have to do is find it, take some, and share the rest. Sometimes, life is that simple.

Although there were times when I felt that the futile loss of my father and other family members was too much for me to bear, it was my good fortune to escape the death camps of the Holocaust, and I intended to make the most of my life. I'm seventy-one years old now and although I am a Jew who has hardly seen the inside of a synagogue, I still possess a fake Roman Catholic baptismal certificate, and it has been said that I have the luck of the Irish. Every day since the age of six has been precious to me, something to treasure.

Courage To Care

Fighting Prejudice Today

Tomas Fleischmann tours broader communities across Australia promoting respect for cultural differences and emphasises the importance of standing up to racism, persecution and any form of prejudice with Courage to Care, a unique travelling exhibition which stresses, through personal experiences, how a simple act of kindness can save a life.

Courage to Care has been seen by almost a quarter of a million people across Australia.

Responses to the Courage to Care program are remarkable. Students have sent examples of their acts of kindness to their friends, some have cried after hearing a survivor's story, individuals have opened up and revealed aspects of their private life that need attention and assistance, an entire class has apologised to a single student for years of bullying.

If you would like to be inspired by the personal experiences or remarkable individuals who had the courage to risk their lives and the lives of their families to save minorities during times of conflict, if you would like to meet the faces of those who, in the face of inhuman forces destroying lives and societies, took enormous personal risks to rescue those facing peril, including the Righteous Among Nations (individuals awarded for their bravery in assisting and hiding Jews during the Holocaust), or if you would like to meet local heroes who have shown bravery and selflessness in your community, contact Courage to Care today.

The travelling program combating racism and prejudice is supported by the Department of Education and visits major cities and regional areas.

Andrew Havas OAM

Chairman, Courage to Care

For more information please visit www.couragetocare.com.au.